The Jumbo Jokes and Riddles Book for Kids

Over 500 Hilarious Jokes, Riddles and Brain Teasers Fun for The Whole Family

DL Digital Entertainment
MADE TO ENTERTAIN

DL Digital Entertainment

TABLE OF CONTENTS

Name _____

Unscramble the words and write them on the lines.

t j e	p n e
t e p	e n t
n m e	e w t
n e h	n t e

Circle the words that are not used above.

jet	den	Ben	wet	men
ten	pen	net	then	pet
set	met	bet	hen	get

CD-3726

Name _____

Write each word three times.

bed _____

fed _____

Ted _____

sled _____

bell _____

fell _____

well _____

yell _____

Name _____

Cut out the pictures. Paste them next to the correct words.

sled

well

bell

fed

bed

yell

fell

Ted

Name _____

Unscramble the words and write them on the lines.

e s l d	e l y l
l f e l	b d e
d e r	b l e l
l l w e	e d f

Circle the words that are not used above.

Ted	red	led	well	bed
sled	bell	sell	fell	cell
tell	fed	Ned	wed	yell

Name _____

Write each word three times.

fin

pin

tin

win

big

dig

pig

wig

Name _____

Cut out the pictures. Paste them next to the correct words.

dig   pin

tin   pig

big   win

fin   wig

Name _____

Unscramble the words and write them on the lines.

g i p	i n f
n w i	b g i
g w i	n i p
i n t	d g i

Circle the words that are not used above.

fig	big	grin	tin	rig
win	pin	twin	dig	zig
spin	wig	pig	twig	fin

Name _____

Write each word three times.

hip

_____

lip

_____

rip

_____

zip

_____

bill

_____

fill

_____

hill

_____

pill

_____

Name _____

Cut out the pictures. Paste them next to the correct words.

lip

fill

hill

hip

rip

bill

pill

zip

Name _____

Unscramble the words and write them on the lines.

l i b l	p i r
p h i	i l l f
l h i l	i p l
p z i	p l l i

Circle the words that are not used above.

pill	zip	hip	dill	hill
will	tip	mill	bill	dip
nip	fill	rip	gill	lip

CD-3726

Name _____

Write each word three times.

cot _____

dot _____

hot _____

pot _____

hop _____

mop _____

pop _____

top _____

         CD-3726

Name _____

Cut out the pictures. Paste them next to the correct words.

hot   hop

mop   dot

cot   top

pop   pot

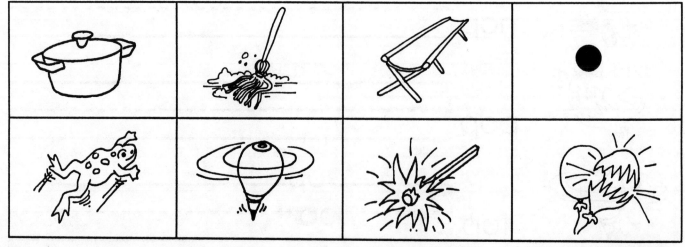

Name _____

Unscramble the words and write them on the lines.

p t o	o p p
t h o	t o d
p h o	t c o
o p t	o m p

Circle the words that are not used above.

pop	cot	got	hop	jot
bop	mop	cop	dot	lot
pot	hot	top	not	stop

Name _____

Write each word three times.

dog _____

hog _____

jog _____

log _____

Bob _____

cob _____

rob _____

sob _____

Name _____

Cut out the pictures. Paste them next to the correct words.

cob

hog

log

rob

Bob

jog

dog

sob

Skill: short o words -og -ob

Name _____

Unscramble the words and write them on the lines.

o r b	g j o
o g h	b B o
b o s	b o c
o g l	g d o

Circle the words that are not used above.

dog	mob	rob	fog	gob
bog	clog	hog	cob	job
sob	log	slob	Bob	jog

Name _____

Write each word three times.

cub _____

rub _____

sub _____

tub _____

bug _____

jug _____

rug _____

tug _____

Name _____

Cut out the pictures. Paste them next to the correct words.

bug   tub

sub   jug

rug   rub

cub   tug

26

Name _____

Unscramble the words and write them on the lines.

u g r	b u r
g b u	b t u
b u s	u g j
t g u	u c b

Circle the words that are not used above.

nub	bug	rub	dug	pub
cub	hug	jug	hub	sub
tug	tub	lug	rug	mug

Name_____

Write each word three times.

gum _____

drum _____

mum _____

plum _____

bump _____

hump _____

jump _____

pump _____

Name _____

Cut out the pictures. Paste them next to the correct words.

jump   drum

gum   bump

hump   plum

mum   pump

Name _____

Unscramble the words and write them on the lines.

m l u p	p u p m
m u j p	m u g
u m d r	p m b u
m m u	m u h p

Circle the words that are not used above.

plum	drum	dump	jump	bum
bump	chum	lump	gum	sum
stump	hump	mum	hum	pump

Name

Write each word three times.

face

_____

lace

_____

race

_____

space

_____

bake

_____

cake

_____

lake

_____

rake

_____

Name _____

Cut out the pictures. Match them to the words and paste.

space   rake

cake   lace

race   bake

lake   face

Name _____

Unscramble the words and write them on the lines.

c e a k	a c e f
k l a e	c e a r
c a l e	a k e r
k e a b	s c a e p

Circle the words that were not used above.

face	bake	pace	fake	race
place	rake	make	ace	lake
space	sake	lace	cake	take

CD-3726

Name _____

Write each word three times.

gate _____

mate _____

plate _____

skate _____

mail _____

nail _____

pail _____

sail _____

Name _____

Cut out the pictures. Match them to the words and paste.

pail   mate

skate   mail

nail   plate

gate   sail

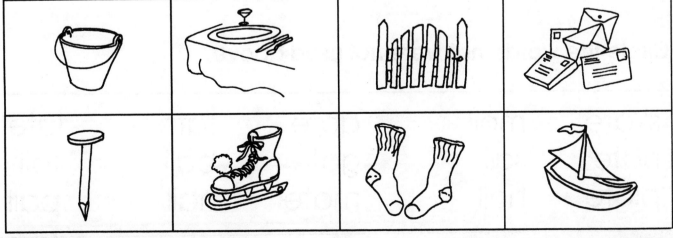

Name _____

Unscramble the words and write them on the lines.

t e m a	a n i l
a p l i	l a s i
t l a p e	t a g e
m a l i	k a s t e

Circle the words that were not used above.

skate	mail	date	fate	late
hate	sail	gate	bail	fail
plate	hail	mate	nail	pail

Skill: long e words -eam -ear

Name ______________________

Write each word three times.

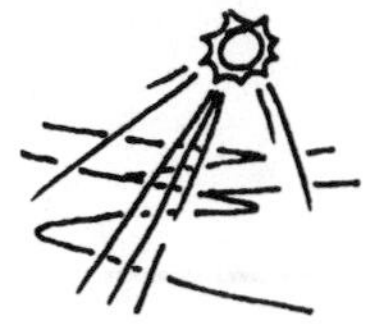

beam

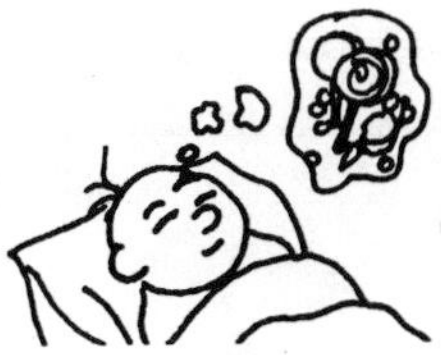

dream

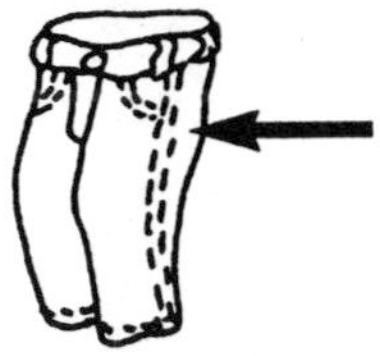

seam

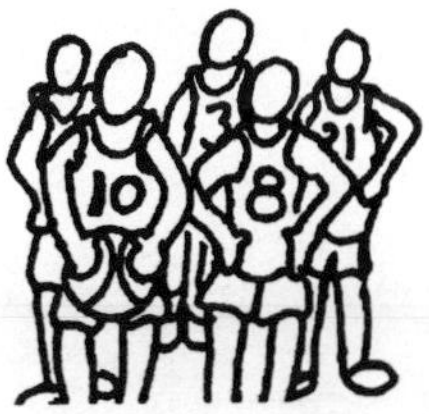

team

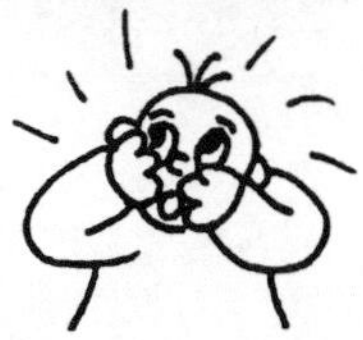

fear

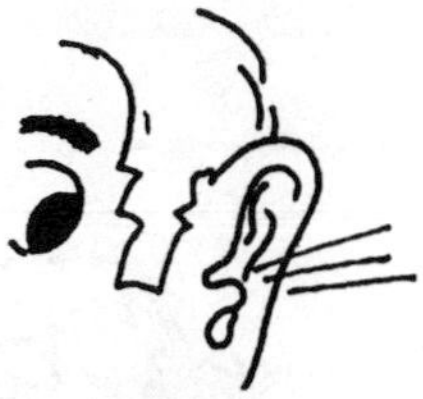

hear

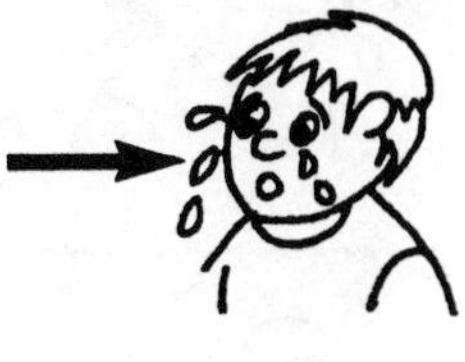

tear

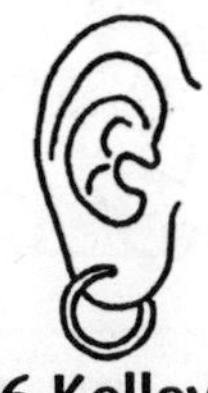

ear

Name _____

Cut out the pictures. Match them to the words and paste.

seam

hear

ear

team

dream

fear

tear

beam

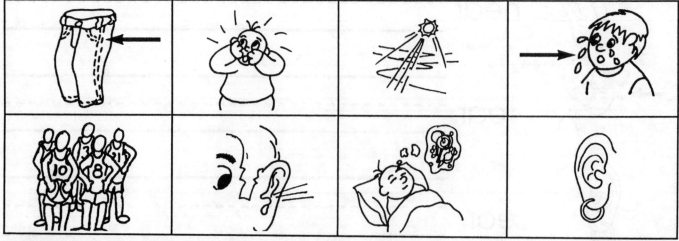

38

Name _____

Unscramble the words and write them on the lines.

r e t a	a e s m
r e a f	m e a r d
y r e a	a h e r
t a e m	m a e b

Circle the words that were not used above.

fear	cream	seam	gear	near
dear	beam	steam	year	ear
dream	hear	tear	clear	team

Name _____

Write each word three times.

reed _____

seed _____

speed _____

weed _____

deep _____

jeep _____

sheep _____

sleep _____

Name _____

Cut out the pictures. Match them to the words and paste.

seed

jeep

sheep

speed

weed

deep

sleep

reed

Name _____

Unscramble the words and write them on the lines.

e e h s p	e e s d
e p d e	d e r e
s e p e d	w e d e
l e p e s	p e j e

Circle the words that were not used above.

weed	deed	deep	keep	seed
feed	speed	peep	need	seep
heed	sheep	reed	sleep	jeep

Name _____

Write each word three times.

dice _____

mice _____

rice _____

price _____

line _____

nine _____

pine _____

vine _____

Name _____

Cut out the pictures. Match them to the words and paste.

line   rice

dice   pine

nine   price

mice   vine

Name _____

Unscramble the words and write them on the lines.

n e v i	c r i e
d e i c	i n n e
n i p e	p i e r c
i c e m	n i l e

Circle the words that were not used above.

pine	fine	dice	nice	mine
ice	line	slice	wine	vine
price	dine	nine	mice	rice

Name _____

Write each word three times.

dive _____

drive _____

five _____

hive _____

hide _____

ride _____

slide _____

tide _____

Name

Cut out the pictures. Match them to the words and paste.

tide   hive

drive   hide

ride   five

dive   slide

Name _____

Unscramble the words and write them on the lines.

d i l s e	v i f e
e d i w	d i r e
e v i h	v i r e d
d i e h	e i v d

Circle the words that were not used above.

wide	hive	live	pride	alive
side	five	slide	tide	dive
drive	ride	bride	hide	chive

Name _____

Write each word three times.

boat _____

coat _____

goat _____

moat _____

cold _____

fold _____

gold _____

hold _____

49 CD-3726

Name _____

Cut out the pictures. Match them to the words and paste.

gold   goat

boat   fold

hold   moat

coat   cold

Name _____

Unscramble the words and write them on the lines.

t o c a	d o l f
a t o b	o a t m
o l d h	l o c d
t o a g	d o l g

Circle the words that were not used above.

float	gold	oat	moat	cold
boat	told	coat	hold	bold
mold	fold	goat	sold	old

Name _____

Write each word three times.

bone _____

cone _____

phone _____

stone _____

core _____

tore _____

shore _____

store _____

Name_____

Cut out the pictures. Match them to the words and paste.

tore

phone

bone

store

core

stone

cone

shore

Name _____

Unscramble the words and write them on the lines.

n o p h e	r o c e
o n c e	t r o e
s o h e r	o n s e t
o r t e s	n e o b

Circle the words that were not used above.

bone	more	pore	lore	stone
core	cone	shore	lone	tone
phone	tore	sore	store	bore

Name _____

Write each word three times.

cube _____

flute _____

fruit _____

fuel _____

huge _____

mule _____

music _____

ruler _____

Name_____

Cut out the pictures. Match them to the words and paste.

fuel   flute

music   ruler

mule   cube

huge   fruit

Name _____

Unscramble the words and write them on the lines.

u h g e	l u e m
_____ - - - - - - - - - - _____	_____ - - - - - - - - - - _____
t i u f r	t u c e
_____ - - - - - - - - - - _____	_____ - - - - - - - - - - _____
b c e u	s c u i m
_____ - - - - - - - - - - _____	_____ - - - - - - - - - - _____
l e f u	l e r u r
_____ - - - - - - - - - - _____	_____ - - - - - - - - - - _____

Circle the words that were not used above.

fuel	cube	use	fruit	rule
fume	music	fuse	ruler	mule
future	cute	huge	fume	plume

Name _____

Write each word three times.

blue _____

cute _____

glue _____

prune _____

suit _____

super _____

tube _____

tune _____

Name _____

Cut out the pictures. Match them to the words and paste.

tune   glue

super   prune

blue   tube

cute   suit

Name _____

Unscramble the words and write them on the lines.

t n u e	u l g e
p r u s e	n u p r e
e u b l	u i t s
b u t e	t u f l e

Circle the words that were not used above.

flute	tuna	ruin	glue	prune
dune	rude	tune	duty	future
suit	tube	blue	human	super

60

Name _____

Write the missing vowel for each picture.

b __ t   h __ n   f __ n

c __ t   c __ b   c __ n

j __ t   b __ g   h __ p

b __ g   b __ g   b __ d

Name _____

Write the missing vowel for each picture.

h __ p	d __ g	g __ m
b __ ll	b __ ll	h __ t
t __ n	b __ mp	c __ t
m __ n	p __ n	d __ t

Name _____

Write the missing vowel for each picture.

r __ b   f __ n   n __ t

d __ g   m __ p   j __ g

r __ g   f __ d   l __ p

h __ g   d r __ m   f __ ll

Name _____

Write the missing vowel for each picture.

f __ ll	f __ ll	c __ b
h __ mp	f __ t	p __ n
t __ n	h __ t	s __ b
m __ n	p __ t	p __ g

Name _____

Write the missing vowel for each picture.

p __ p	r __ g	t __ g
r __ d	r __ p	j __ g
m __ m	t __ ll	w __ ll
h __ ll	r __ b	j __ m p

Name _____

Write the missing vowel for each picture.

f __ c e	b __ a m	d __ c e
b __ a t	c __ b e	b __ k e
f __ a r	l __ n e	c __ l d
h __ g e	g __ t e	r __ e d

Name _____

Write the missing vowel for each picture.

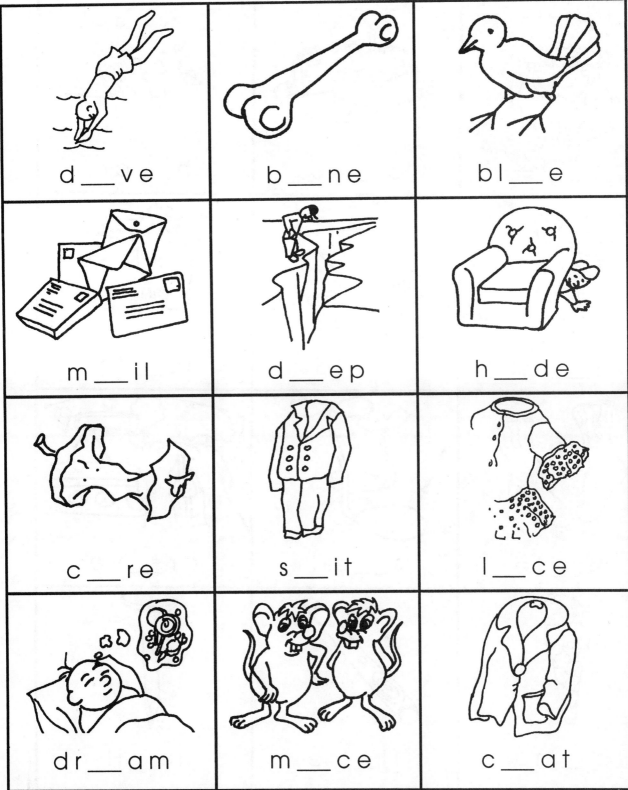

d __ ve

b __ ne

bl __ e

m __ il

d __ ep

h __ de

c __ re

s __ it

l __ ce

dr __ am

m __ ce

c __ at

Name _____

Write the missing vowel for each picture.

c __ te	c __ ke	h __ ar
n __ ne	f __ ld	m __ le
m __ te	s __ ed	dr __ ve
c __ ne	fl __ te	n __ il

Name _____

Write the missing vowel for each picture.

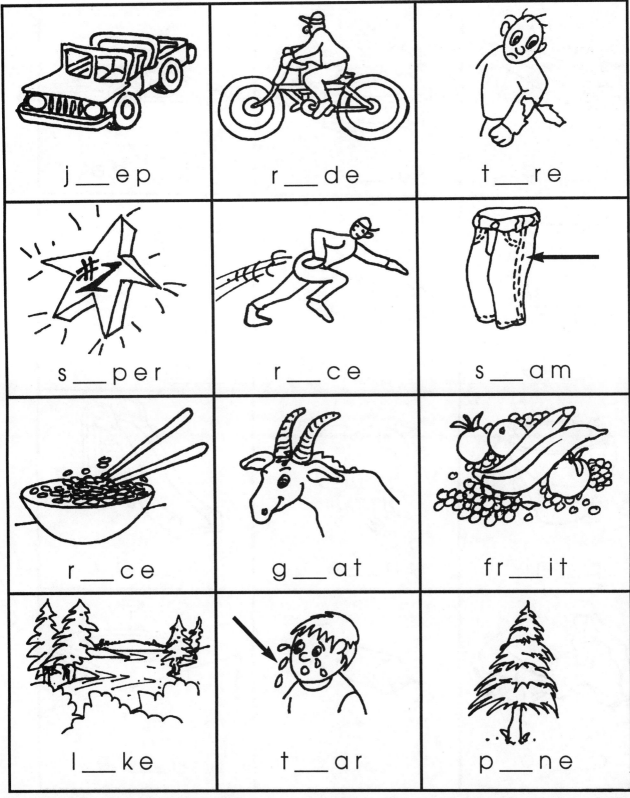

j__ep

r__de

t__re

s__per

r__ce

s__am

r__ce

g__at

fr__it

l__ke

t__ar

p__ne

Name _____

Write the missing vowel for each picture.

g __ ld

m __ sic

sp __ ed

f __ ve

ph __ ne

gl __ e

p __ il

sh __ ep

sl __ de

c __ re

t __ be

pl __ te

Name _____

Write the missing vowel for each picture.

w___n	sp___ce	p___t
t___am	t___b	pr___ce
p___n	m___at	w___t
f___el	w___g	r___ke

Name _____

Write the missing vowel for each picture.

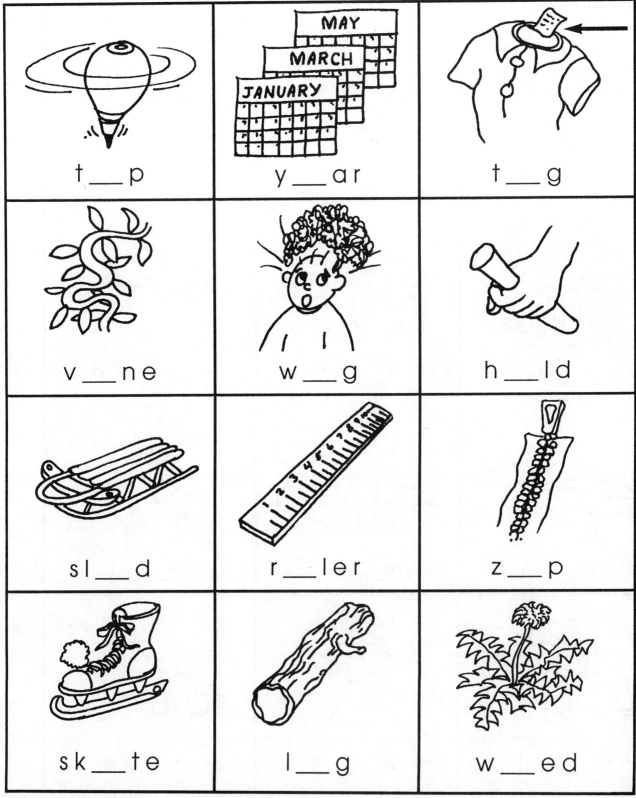

t __ p

y __ a r

t __ g

v __ n e

w __ g

h __ l d

s l __ d

r __ l e r

z __ p

s k __ t e

l __ g

w __ e d

72   CD-3726

Name _____

Write the missing vowel for each picture.

pl __ m   h __ ve   w __ ll

st __ ne   y __ ll   pr __ ne

p __ ll   s __ il   s __ b

sl __ ep   p __ mp   st __ re

Name _____

Choose the answer that makes sense then write it on the line.

1. A _____ can fly.   **bat**   **cat**

2. Please _____ my back.   **rib**   **rub**

3. That _____ is my father.   **men**   **man**

4. It is _____ today.   **hot**   **hat**

5. Put the lunch in a _____ .   **big**   **bag**

6. I will _____ to school.   **jog**   **jug**

7. Some apples are _____ .   **red**   **rod**

8. Play _____ with me.   **ball**   **bell**

9. My _____ is a dog.   **pat**   **pet**

10. The puppy will _____ his tail. **wig**   **wag**

Write the answers that have a short a sound here.

Name _____

Choose the answer that makes sense then write it on the line.

1. Do not _____ down!   **fall**   **fell**

2. A fish has a _____.   **fun**   **fin**

3. A _____ ate the cheese.   **sat**   **rat**

4. Do not _____ my paper.   **rip**   **lip**

5. A _____ makes wind.   **fin**   **fan**

6. A camel has one _____.   **hump**   **jump**

7. A rabbit can _____.   **hop**   **hip**

8. I can _____ a big hole.   **dig**   **dug**

9. I play a _____ in the band.   **gum**   **drum**

10. I will _____ the race.   **won**   **win**

Write the answers that have a short a sound here.

Name _____

Choose the answer that makes sense then write it on the line.

1. The _____ is on the floor.　　rug　　rag

2. Are you feeling _____ ?　　well　　will

3. That is a _____ tree.　　tell　　tall

4. A _____ flys over clouds.　　jot　　jet

5. The _____ has two chicks.　　hen　　men

6. Spot is the name of my _____.　　dig　　dog

7. I got _____ in the rain.　　wet　　met

8. _____ my cup to the top.　　Fill　　Fall

9. I will go to _____ now.　　bed　　bad

10. Fry the eggs in that _____.　　pin　　pan

Write the answers that have a short e sound here.

Name _____

Choose the answer that makes sense then write it on the line.

1. We _____ the horse oats.   **fed**   **bed**

2. Ring the _____ .   **ball**   **bell**

3. Let's play _____ .   **bag**   **tag**

4. I like corn on the _____ .   **cob**   **mob**

5. Put a _____ on the fire.   **log**   **jog**

6. I will eat a _____ .   **mum**   **plum**

7. Can you _____ very high?   **jump**   **stump**

8. That is a _____ ball!   **beg**   **big**

9. Mother will _____ the floor.   **stop**   **mop**

10. My _____ is in the tent.   **cot**   **cut**

Write the answers that have a short e sound here.

Name _____

Choose the answer that makes sense then write it on the line.

1. A _____ just flew by.

big   bug

2. Let's climb that _____.

hill   hall

3. My _____ goes in the snow.

slid   sled

4. Joe just _____ down.

fell   fill

5. Do not _____ at me.

yell   bell

6. We wash in the _____.

tab   tub

7. I _____ my head.

bumped   jumped

8. Put it on _____ of this.

tap   top

9. I have a _____ cat.

pit   pet

10. I _____ when I get hurt.

mob   sob

Write the answers that have a short i sound here.

Name _____

Choose the answer that makes sense then write it on the line.

1. A _____ can make you well.   **hill**   **pill**

2. Put a _____ over the letter i.   **pot**   **dot**

3. The dog _____ on a rope.   **bugs**   **tugs**

4. _____ the zipper.   **Zip**   **Sip**

5. A _____ is part of a leg.   **hip**   **hop**

6. This old shirt is a _____ .   **rag**   **rig**

7. I have _____ toes.   **tin**   **ten**

8. I like to drink _____ .   **pup**   **pop**

9. Cook soup in a big _____ .   **pet**   **pot**

10. That lady wears a _____ .   **wag**   **wig**

Write the answers that have a short o sound here.

Name _____

Choose the answer that makes sense then write it on the line.

1. A _____ is an animal.   **pig**   **peg**

2. I bit my _____ !   **lap**   **lip**

3. A _____ is a flower   **mum**   **gum**

4. A _____ is a baby bear.   **cub**   **cab**

5. Boys grow up to be _____ .   **men**   **hen**

6. I blow bubbles with _____ .   **gum**   **hum**

7. I have a butterfly _____ .   **net**   **nut**

8. Use a _____ , not a pencil.   **ten**   **pen**

9. A _____ goes under water.   **sob**   **sub**

10. _____ air into my bike tires. **Pump**   **Lump**

Write the answers that have a short u sound here.

Name _____

Choose the answer that makes sense then write it on the line.

1. _____ the wood together.   **Sail**   **Nail**

2. Leaves grow on a _____ .   **mine**   **vine**

3. _____ grow into plants.   **Needs**   **Seeds**

4. _____ the cake in the oven.   **Bake**   **Bike**

5. The ice cream is _____ .   **cold**   **fold**

6. The _____ is ringing.   **cone**   **phone**

7. I like _____ with my dinner.   **race**   **rice**

8. You did a _____ job!   **super**   **fruit**

9. Put your food on a _____.   **gate**   **plate**

10. Let's have a _____ .   **face**   **race**

Write the answers that have a long a sound here.

Name _____

Choose the answer that makes sense then write it on the line.

1. My nose is on my _____ .   **lace**   **face**

2. I like to _____ on a sled.   **slide**   **wide**

3. Do not eat the apple _____ .   **care**   **core**

4. A_____ helps us draw a line.   **ruler**   **super**

5. Help me _____ this sheet.   **cold**   **fold**

6. We can _____ the leaves.   **cake**   **rake**

7. How_____ is the box?   **side**   **wide**

8. Let's swim in the_____ .   **lake**   **make**

9. I am _____ years old.   **fine**   **nine**

10. Put the water in a _____ .   **pail**   **mail**

Write the answers that have a long a sound here.

82   CD-3726

Name _____

Choose the answer that makes sense then write it on the line.

1. I had a _____ last night.   **dream**   **seam**

2. The _____ are in the barn.   **sheep**   **sleep**

3. That boat has a _____ .   **sail**   **tail**

4. Stars are out in _____ .   **spice**   **space**

5. A _____ is a small rock.   **bone**   **stone**

6. Roll the _____ and play.   **dice**   **slice**

7. I _____ we may be late.   **tear**   **fear**

8. I like chocolate _____ .   **cake**   **make**

9. _____ and I will find you.   **Side**   **Hide**

10. My paper _____ in half.   **tore**   **tire**

Write the answers that have a long e sound here.

Name _____

Choose the answer that makes sense then write it on the line.

1. I can _____ into the pool.　　five　　dive

2. Do you _____ the band?　　hear　　tear

3. A _____ is like a horse.　　mule　　mile

4. My ring is made of _____ .　　gold　　hold

5. I have _____ dimes.　　five　　dive

6. Sally is one _____ old.　　dear　　year

7. Can you _____ a car?　　drive　　hive

8. Please be on my _____ .　　steam　　team

9. Close the barnyard _____ .　　gate　　mate

10. Do you play the _____ ?　　flute　　cute

Write the answers that have a long i sound here.

Name _____

Choose the answer that makes sense then write it on the line.

1. The _____ is on the lake.   **boat**   **coat**

2. Wear a _____ to the party.   **fruit**   **suit**

3. Please _____ this letter.   **mail**   **pail**

4. A shell was on the _____ .   **shore**   **share**

5. Let's _____ after school.   **gate**   **skate**

6. The dog has a _____ .   **lone**   **bone**

7. Do not _____ in a car.   **need**   **speed**

8. A _____ is a kind of fruit.   **prune**   **tune**

9. Draw a _____ under this.   **line**   **pine**

10. The _____ ate my lunch!   **moat**   **goat**

Write the answers that have a long o sound here.

Name _____

Choose the answer that makes sense then write it on the line.

1. That is a tall _____ tree.   line   pine

2. The paint comes in a _____ .   cube   tube

3. Use _____ to hold that.   glue   blue

4. Wear a warm _____ today.   coat   boat

5. May I _____ your bike?   side   ride

6. I think you are _____ .   cute   flute

7. Is the water very _____?   keep   deep

8. Please _____ the garden.   need   weed

9. I love to eat _____ .   fruit   suit

10. Gas is a kind of _____ .   fuel   mule

Write the answers that have a long u sound here.

CD-3726

Name _____

Choose the answer that makes sense then write it on the line.

1. I shop in that _____.   **store**   **core**

2. I like to listen to _____.   **ruler**   **music**

3. The cat does not like _____.   **price**   **mice**

4. I need an ice _____.   **cube**   **cute**

5. The bees are in their _____.   **drive**   **hive**

6. _____ on to my hand.   **Gold**   **Hold**

7. I like the color _____.   **blue**   **glue**

8. That shirt is _____ on you!   **huge**   **tube**

9. I _____ in a bed.   **sheep**   **sleep**

10. Play a _____ on your horn.   **tune**   **prune**

_____

Write the answers that have a long u sound here.

Name _____

Put these words into the correct group.

bag	bat	bake	cake
can	fan	face	gate
mate	nail	pan	rag
rake	space	tall	wall

Short a   Long a

_____   _____

_____   _____

_____   _____

_____   _____

_____   _____

_____   _____

Choose five words and draw a picture next to each.

Name _____

Put these words into the correct group.

beam	bed	deep	fear
fell	hen	jeep	jet
men	pet	reed	sled
sleep	team	year	yell

Short e

_____

_____

_____

_____

_____

_____

Long e

_____

_____

_____

_____

_____

_____

Choose five words and draw a picture next to each.

Name _____

Put these words into the correct group.

bill	dice	dig	dive
fin	five	hide	hill
line	lip	pin	price
vine	wide	wig	zip

Short i   ## Long i

_____   _____

_____   _____

_____   _____

_____   _____

_____   _____

_____   _____

_____   _____

Choose five words and draw a picture next to each.

Name _____

Put these words into the correct group.

boat	cob	cone	dot
fold	goat	hold	hop
jog	log	moat	mop
phone	pot	rob	store

Short o	Long o
_____	_____
_____	_____
_____	_____
_____	_____
_____	_____
_____	_____

Choose five words and draw a picture next to each.

Name _____

Put these words into the correct group.

blue	bug	cub	cute
drum	flute	fruit	glue
gum	hump	jug	mule
rub	ruler	tug	tune

Short u

_____

_____

_____

_____

_____

_____

Long u

_____

_____

_____

_____

_____

_____

Choose five words and draw a picture next to each.

Name _____

Put these words into the correct group.

ball	bell	cat	dream
fed	hear	lake	man
net	pail	race	sheep
skate	ten	wag	weed

Short a	Short e
_____	_____
_____	_____
_____	_____

Long a	Long e
_____	_____
_____	_____
_____	_____

Name _____

Put these words into the correct group.

bone	bump	coat	core
cot	cube	dog	huge
mule	plum	rug	sob
stone	suit	top	tub

Short o	Short u
_____	_____
_____	_____
_____	_____
_____	_____

Long o	Long u
_____	_____
_____	_____
_____	_____
_____	_____

Name _____

Fill in the blanks with the short a words in the box.

Sally's Walk

Sally went for a walk down her street. She stopped in front of the house next to hers. A _____ was in the yard. He was feeding his _____. The man went into his house. The cat jumped to the top of a brick _____ that went around the yard. Sally walked on to the next yard. A dog was barking at the cat. He began to _____ his tail when he saw Sally. He got his _____ and tossed it in the air. The dog put the ball at Sally's feet and _____ down. She threw the ball and the dog went after it.   He came back with a paper _____ in his mouth. A _____ on the bag said "Open Me". He gave the bag to _____ and she opened it. _____ you guess what was inside?

bag	ball	Can	cat	man
Sally	sat	tag	wag	wall

Name _____

Fill in the blanks with the short e words at the bottom of the page.

Ned

One summer day Ned went to his uncle's farm. He went to the barnyard to look around. Ned saw a fat _____ and her five babies. He _____ corn to the hen. There were some sheep in a _____ near the barn. A horse and her colt were in the barn. Ned stopped to _____ the soft nose of the colt. Ned walked out of the barn and saw a round stone wall. He looked over the wall and saw that it was a wishing _____ . Ned bent over to see further into the well and _____ in! The water was not very deep, but Ned was all _____ . He began to _____ for help. Two _____ came running. They used a big _____ to pull him out. Ned laughed and said "I am all right now"!

fed	fell	hen	men	net
pen	pet	well	wet	yell

Name_____

Fill in the blanks with the short i words **at** the bottom of the page.

Bill's Pond

Bill was playing in his back yard. He saw a _____

pile of dirt under a bush. It was an ant _____. He had

an idea. He would make a pond for the ants to _____

in. The ants could race and see who would _____ . Bill

began to _____ a small hole next to the ant hill. He

worked on that hole for a long time.   When it was ready he

_____the hole with water. The ants came to the

pond but they did not go _____ .   Bill laughed at his

_____ idea.   Ants cannot swim. They do not have

_____ like fish, but now they_____ have

a nice pond to

look at!

big	dig	filled	fins	hill
in	silly	swim	will	win

Name _____

Fill in the blanks with the short o words **at** the bottom of **the page**.

Friends

Bob and Rob are friends. They are alike in many ways.

Both boys like to climb to the _____ of the fence. Then

they _____ down. They both have a _____

for a pet. They even like the same foods. Their favorite food

is corn on the _____ . Bob and Rob like to drink

_____ chocolate in the winter and cold _____

in the summer. Both boys like to make things. Once they

made a big _____ out of clay. Another time they

made a _____ cabin out of sticks. Bob and

_____ have known each other since they were

two years old. They have been friends for a _____

time!

cob	dog	hop	hot	log
long	pop	pot	Rob	top

Name _____

Fill in the blanks with the short u words **at** the bottom of the page.

My Toy Box

I have a big box to keep my toys in.   It is painted yellow

and green. My box is _____ of toys. At the bottom I

keep an old red _____ for banging. Next I have three

boats and one _____ to play with in the _____.

On top of them I keep two stuffed animals.   One is a camel

with a big _____ .   The other is a small bear

_____ . On the top I keep a real animal!   It is a

_____ with wings and six legs.   My toy box is so full I

have to _____ on the top to open it. Sometimes I pull

the top so hard it flies open and _____ my head.

Then I have to_____ my head to make it feel better.

bug	bumps	cub	drum	full
hump	rub	sub	tub	tug

Name _____

Fill in the blanks with the long a words at the bottom of the page.

Amy's Party

Amy is having a party today. She _____ letters

to all her friends last week to tell them about it. Amy has put

on her best dress. It has _____ all over it. Her

mother has _____ a _____ for the

children to eat. They will put the cake on party _____ .

Amy has _____ many plans for her party. The

children will play _____ . They will have a running

_____ . They may even _____ boats on

the nearby pond! The doorbell rings. It is the first guest.

Amy has a big smile on her _____ .

baked	cake	face	games	lace
made	mailed	plates	race	sail

Name_____

Fill in the blanks with the long e words at the bottom of the page.

A Dream by the Sea

Last week Lee went camping with her family. They went to a camp by the sea. They knew it was a nice place because they went there last _____. The camp has a nice beach for swimming. _____ likes to swim in water that is not too _____. She is not a good swimmer. The family likes to camp by the _____. They have a _____ to drive over the sand dunes. They _____ in a tent. Lee likes to _____ the waves at night. One night she had a _____. She found a large _____ and planted it. A giant_____ grew from the seed. It became a sea weed. What a strange dream!

dream	deep	hear	jeep	Lee
sea	seed	sleep	weed	year

Name _____

Fill in the blanks with the long i words at the bottom of the page.

The Woods

Mike and Ivan like to picnic in the woods. It takes them only _____ minutes to get there. They like to _____ their _____ down the trails. There are many _____ trees in the woods. Some of them are covered with _____ that are just right for swinging from. One tree is so _____ the boys cannot put their arms around it! Mike and Ivan like to _____ in the bushes and watch for animals. They often see little _____ gathering seeds. Once they saw some bees going into a large _____ . The woods are _____ with small animals that are fun to watch.

alive	bikes	five	hide	hive
pine	mice	ride	vines	wide

Name_____

Fill in the blanks with the long o words at the bottom of the page.

Gold Fish

Once a boy named Joe lived near a castle. There was a

_____ around the castle and Joe liked to fish there.

He had a small _____ to fish from.   The boat

_____ on the water as Joe fished. _____

caught one fish each day for his dinner. One winter morning

it was very _____ out. Joe put on his _____

and went to the moat.   His fingers were so cold he could

barely _____ the oars.   He pushed away from

the _____ and began to fish. He looked down

and saw a shiny _____ in the water. Joe picked it

up and saw that it was a big piece of _____ .

He had found gold instead of a fish. What a lucky day!

boat	coat	cold	floated	gold
hold	Joe	moat	shore	stone

Name_____

Fill in the blanks with the long u words **at** the bottom **of** the page.

Ruth's Flute

Ruth likes school. She loves _____ class better

than anything. She plays a _____ in the band. Her

teacher says she is a _____ student. She can

play a _____ without looking at the music!

_____ is learning to write her own songs. She uses a

_____ to make the lines then draws in the notes.

Ruth will play at a school program tonight. She puts on her

best _____ so she will look nice. It is the color of a

_____ sky. Her father says she looks _____ .

There is a _____ crowd at the school. Ruth

plays well and everyone claps.

blue	cute	flute	huge	music
ruler	Ruth	suit	super	tune

Super Reader Award

_____

receives this award for

_____

Keep up the great work!

_____ _____
signed   date

Reading Award

_____

receives this award for

_____

Great Job!

_____ _____
signed   date

CD-3726

Answer Key

Name _____

Skill: short a words -an -at

Write each word three times.

bat _____

cat _____

fat _____

mat _____

can _____

fan _____

man _____

pan _____

1

Name _____

Skill: short a words -an -at

Cut out the pictures. Paste them next to the correct words.

can   cat

bat   man

pan   mat

fan   hat

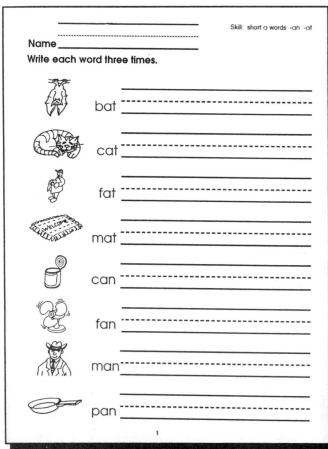

pan	fan	bat	man
mat	cat	can	hat

2

Name _____

Skill: short a words -an -at

Unscramble the words and write them on the lines.

t m a	a h t
mat	hat
a n m	p n a
man	pan
n f a	a c t
fan	cat
t a b	n a c
bat	can

Circle the words that are not used above.

(fat)   (ban)   (rat)   can   man
fan   mat   cat   bat   (van)
hat   (sat)   pan   (tan) (ran)

3

Name _____

Skill: short a words -ag -all

Write each word three times.

bag _____

rag _____

tag _____

wag _____

ball _____

fall _____

tall _____

wall _____

4

106
CD-3726

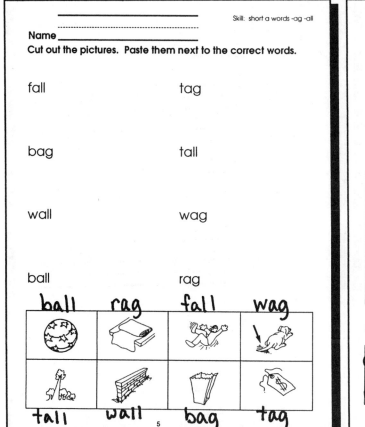

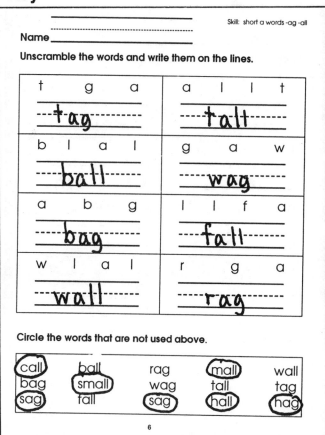

Top Left Worksheet

Skill: short a words -ag -all

Name _____

Cut out the pictures. Paste them next to the correct words.

fall   tag

bag   tall

wall   wag

ball   rag

ball   rag   fall   wag

(ball)	(rag)	(fall)	(wag)
(tall)	(wall)	(bag)	(tag)

tall   wall   bag   tag

5

Top Right Worksheet

Skill: short a words -ag -all

Name _____

Unscramble the words and write them on the lines.

t g a	a l l t
tag	tall
b l a l	g a w
ball	wag
a b g	l l f a
bag	fall
w l a l	r g a
wall	rag

Circle the words that are not used above.

(call)   ball   rag   (mall)   wall
bag   (small)   wag   tall   tag
(sag)   fall   (sag)   (hall)   (hag)

6

Bottom Left Worksheet

Skill: short e words -en -et

Name _____

Write each word three times.

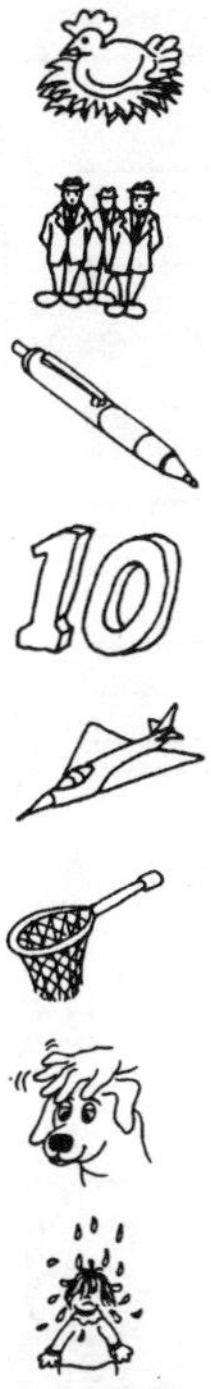

hen _____

men _____

pen _____

ten _____

jet _____

net _____

pet _____

wet _____

7

Bottom Right Worksheet

Skill: short e words -en -et

Name _____

Cut out the pictures. Paste them next to the correct words.

pet   men

ten   jet

wet   hen

pen   net

jet   pen   pet   wet

(jet)	(pen)	(pet)	(wet)
(men)	(hen)	(net)	(ten)

men   hen   net   ten

8

CD-3726

Answer Key

Page 9

Name _____

Skill: short e words -en -et

Unscramble the words and write them on the lines.

t j e	p n e
jet	pen
t e p	e n t
pet	net/ten
n m e	e w t
men	wet
n e h	n t e
hen	ten/net

Circle the words that are not used above.

jet	(den)	(Ben)	wet	men
ten	pen	net	(them)	pet
(set)	(met)	(bet)	hen	(get)

9

Page 10

Name _____

Skill: short e words -ed -ell

Write each word three times.

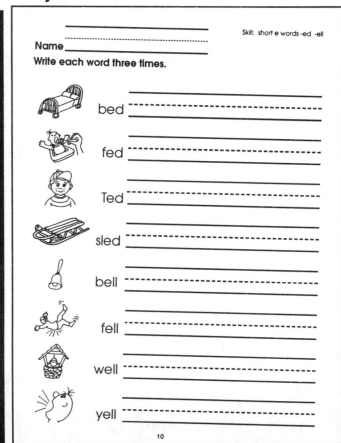

bed _____

fed _____

Ted _____

sled _____

bell _____

fell _____

well _____

yell _____

10

Page 11

Name _____

Skill: short e words -ed -ell

Cut out the pictures. Paste them next to the correct words.

sled   well

bell   fed

bed   yell

fell   Ted

fed   well   bed   Ted

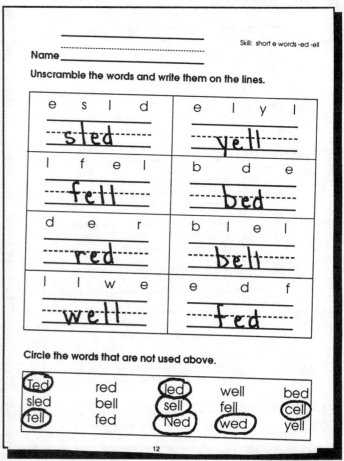

yell   sled   bell   fell

11

Page 12

Name _____

Skill: short e words -ed -ell

Unscramble the words and write them on the lines.

e s l d	e l y l
sled	yell
l f e l	b d e
fell	bed
d e r	b l e l
red	bell
l l w e	e d f
well	fed

Circle the words that are not used above.

(Ted)	red	(led)	well	bed
sled	bell	(sell)	fell	(cell)
(tell)	fed	(Ned)	(wed)	yell

12

Answer Key

Worksheet (page 13)

Name _____

Skill: short i words -in -ig

Write each word three times.

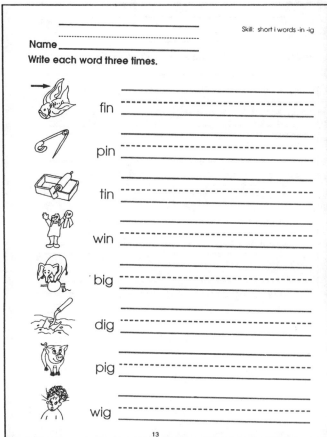

fin _____

pin _____

tin _____

win _____

big _____

dig _____

pig _____

wig _____

13

Worksheet (page 14)

Name _____

Skill: short i words -in -ig

Cut out the pictures. Paste them next to the correct words.

dig   pin

tin   pig

big   win

fin   wig

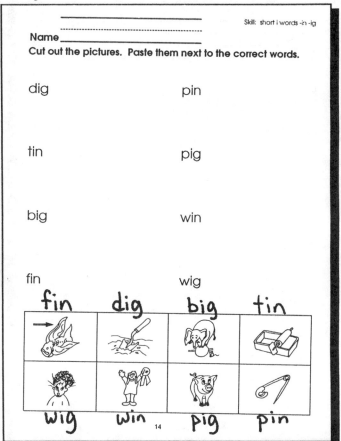

fin   dig   big   tin

wig   win   pig   pin

14

Worksheet (page 15)

Name _____

Skill: short i words -in -ig

Unscramble the words and write them on the lines.

g i p	p i n f
pig	fin
n w i	b g i
win	big
g w i	n i p
wig	pin
i n t	d g i
tin	dig

Circle the words that are not used above.

(fig)   big   (grin)   tin   (rig)
(win)   pin   (twin)   dig   (zig)
(spin) wig   pig   (twig) fin

15

Worksheet (page 16)

Name _____

Skill: short i words -ip -ill

Write each word three times.

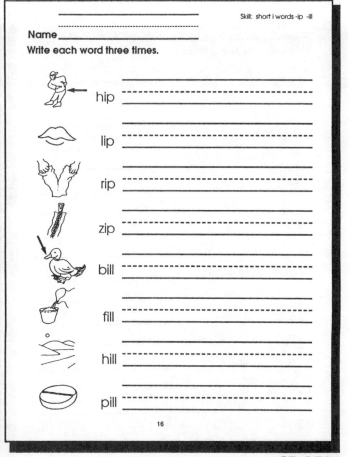

hip _____

lip _____

rip _____

zip _____

bill _____

fill _____

hill _____

pill _____

16

109   CD-3726

Answer Key

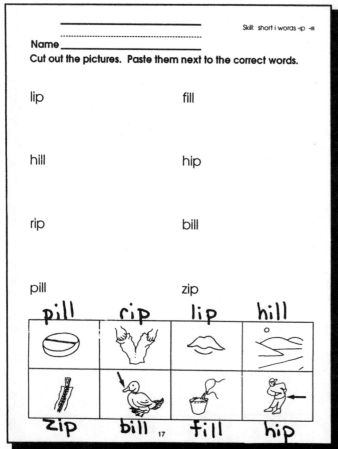

Name _____

Skill: short i words -ip -ill

Cut out the pictures. Paste them next to the correct words.

lip   fill

hill   hip

rip   bill

pill   zip

pill	rip	lip	hill
zip	bill	fill	hip

17

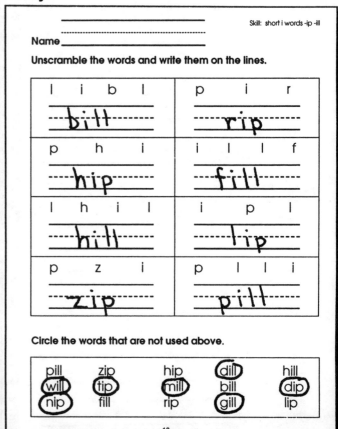

Name _____

Skill: short i words -ip -ill

Unscramble the words and write them on the lines.

l i b l	p i r
bill	rip
p h i	i l l f
hip	fill
l h i l	i p l
hill	lip
p z i	p l l i
zip	pill

Circle the words that are not used above.

pill	zip	hip	dill	hill
will	tip	mill	bill	dip
nip	fill	rip	gill	lip

18

Name _____

Skill: short o words -ot -op

Write each word three times.

cot _____

dot _____

hot _____

pot _____

hop _____

mop _____

pop _____

top _____

19

Name _____

Skill: short o words -ot -op

Cut out the pictures. Paste them next to the correct words.

hot   hop

mop   dot

cot   top

pop   pot

pot	mop	cot	dot
hop	top	hot	pop

20

© 1996 Kelley Wingate Publications   110   CD-3726

Answer Key

Page 21

Name _____

Skill: short o words -ot -op

Unscramble the words and write them on the lines.

p t o	o p p
pot / top	pop
t h o	t o d
hot	dot
p h o	t c o
hop	cot
o p t	o m p
top / pot	mop

Circle the words that are not used above.

pop	cot	(got)	hop	(jot)
(bop)	mop	(cop)	dot	(lot)
pot	hot	(top)	(not)	(stop)

21

Page 22

Name _____

Skill: short o words -og -ob

Write each word three times.

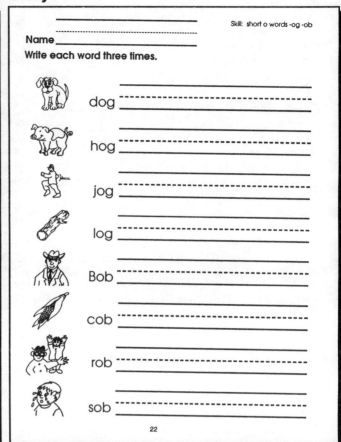

dog _____

hog _____

jog _____

log _____

Bob _____

cob _____

rob _____

sob _____

22

Page 23

Name _____

Skill: short o words -og -ob

Cut out the pictures. Paste them next to the correct words.

cob   hog

log   rob

Bob   jog

dog   sob

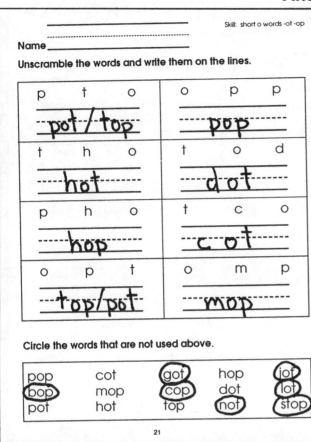

jog	Bob	dog	cob
log	rob	sob	hog

23

Page 24

Name _____

Skill: short o words -og -ob

Unscramble the words and write them on the lines.

o r b	g j o
rob	jog
o g h	b B o
hog	Bob
b o s	b o c
sob	cob
o g l	g d o
log	dog

Circle the words that are not used above.

dog	(mob)	rob	(fog)	(gob)
(bog)	(clog)	hog	cob	(job)
sob	log	(slob)	Bob	jog

24

111

CD-3726

Page 25

Name _____

Skill: short u words -ub -ug

Write each word three times.

cub _____

rub _____

sub _____

tub _____

bug _____

jug _____

rug _____

tug _____

25

Page 26

Name _____

Skill: short u words -ub -ug

Cut out the pictures. Paste them next to the correct words.

bug   tub

sub   jug

rug   rub

cub   tug

tub	jug	cub	tug

rug   sub   bug   rub

26

Page 27

Name _____

Skill: short u words -ub -ug

Unscramble the words and write them on the lines.

u g r	b u r
rug	rub
g b u	b t u
bug	tub
b u s	u g j
sub	jug
t g u	u c b
tug	cub

Circle the words that are not used above.

(nub)   bug   rub   (dug)   (pub)
cub   (hug)   jug   (hub)   sub
tug   tub   (lug)   rug   (mug)

27

Page 28

Name _____

Skill: short u words -um -ump

Write each word three times.

gum _____

drum _____

mum _____

plum _____

bump _____

hump _____

jump _____

pump _____

28

Worksheet (page 29)

Name _____

Skill: short u words -um -ump

Cut out the pictures. Paste them next to the correct words.

jump   drum

gum   bump

hump   plum

mum   pump

jump   drum   pump   hump

gum   plum   bump   mum

Worksheet (page 30)

Name _____

Skill: short u words -um -ump

Unscramble the words and write them on the lines.

m l u p	p u p m
plum	pump
m u j p	m u g
jump	gum
u m d r	p m b u
drum	bump
m m u	m u h p
mum	hump

Circle the words that are not used above.

plum   drum   (dump)   jump   (bum)
bump   (chum)   (lump)   gum   (sum)
(stump) hump   mum   (hum)   pump

Worksheet (page 31)

Name _____

Skill: long a words -ace -ake

Write each word three times.

face _____

lace _____

race _____

space _____

bake _____

cake _____

lake _____

rake _____

Worksheet (page 32)

Name _____

Skill: long a words -ace -ake

Cut out the pictures. Match them to the words and paste.

space   rake

cake   lace

race   bake

lake   face

face   cake   bake   lace

rake   space   lake   race

113

CD-3726

Answer Key

Name _____
Skill: long a words -a

Unscramble the words and write them on the lines.

c e a k	a c e f
cake	face
k l a e	c e a r
take	race
c a l e	a k e r
lace	rake
k e a b	s c a e p
bake	space

Circle the words that were not used above.

face	bake	(pace)	(fake)	race
(place)	rake	(make)	(ace)	lake
space	(sake)	lace	cake	(take)

33

Name _____
Skill: long a words -ate -ail

Write each word three times.

gate _____

mate _____

plate _____

skate _____

mail _____

nail _____

pail _____

sail _____

34

Name _____
Skill: long a words -ate -ail

Cut out the pictures. Match them to the words and paste.

pail   mate

skate   mail

nail   plate

gate   sail

pail	plate	gate	mail
nail	skate	mate	sail

35

Name _____
Skill: long a words -ate -ail

Unscramble the words and write them on the lines.

t e m a	a n i l
mate	nail
a p l i	l a s i
pail	sail
t l a p e	t a g e
plate	gate
m a l i	k a s t e
mail	skate

Circle the words that were not used above.

skate	mail	(date)	(fate)	(late)
(hate)	sail	gate	(bail)	(fail)
plate	(nail)	mate	nail	pail

36

CD-3726

Page 37

Name _____

Skill: long e words -eam -ear

Write each word three times.

beam _____

dream _____

seam _____

team _____

fear _____

hear _____

tear _____

ear _____

37

Page 38

Name _____

Skill: long e words -eam -ear

Cut out the pictures. Match them to the words and paste.

seam   hear

ear   team

dream   fear

tear   beam

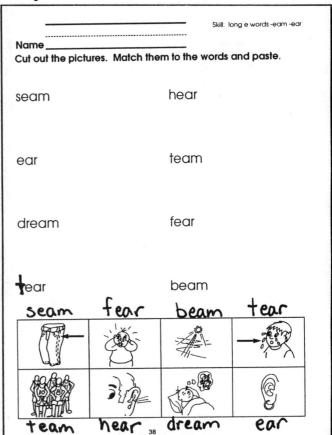

seam	fear	beam	tear
team	hear	dream	ear

38

Page 39

Name _____

Skill: long e words -eam -ear

Unscramble the words and write them on the lines.

r e t a	a e s m
tear	seam
r e a f	m e a r d
fear	dream
y r e a	a h e r
year	hear
t a e m	m a e b
team	beam

Circle the words that were not used above.

fear   (cream)   seam   (gear)   (near)
(dear)   beam   (steam)   year   (ear)
dream   hear   tear   (clear)   team

39

Page 40

Name _____

Skill: long e words -eed -eep

Write each word three times.

reed _____

seed _____

speed _____

weed _____

deep _____

jeep _____

sheep _____

sleep _____

40

Worksheet 1 (page 41)

Name _____

Skill: long e words -eed -eep

Cut out the pictures. Match them to the words and paste.

seed   jeep

sheep   speed

weed   deep

sleep   reed

reed   deep   sheep   speed

seed   sleep   jeep   weed

41

Worksheet 2 (page 42)

Name _____

Skill: long e words -eed -eep

Unscramble the words and write them on the lines.

e e h s p	e e s d
sheep	seed
e p d e	d e r e
deep	reed
s e p e d	w e d e
speed	weed
l e p e s	p e j e
sleep	jeep

Circle the words that were not used above.

weed (deed) deep (keep) seed
(feed) speed (peep) (need) (seep)
(need) sheep reed sleep jeep

42

Worksheet 3 (page 43)

Name _____

Skill: long i words -ice -ine

Write each word three times.

dice _____

mice _____

rice _____

price _____

line _____

nine _____

pine _____

vine _____

43

Worksheet 4 (page 44)

Name _____

Skill: long i words -ice -ine

Cut out the pictures. Match them to the words and paste.

line   rice

dice   pine

nine   price

mice   vine

vine   line   dice   mice

price   rice   pine   nine

44

Page 45

Name _____   Skill: long i words -ice -ine

Unscramble the words and write them on the lines.

n e v i → **vine**	c r i e → **rice**
d e i c → **dice**	i n n e → **nine**
n i p e → **pine**	p i e r c → **price**
i c e m → **mice**	n i l e → **line**

Circle the words that were not used above.

pine (fine) dice (nice) (mine)
(ice) line (slice) (wine) vine
price (dine) nine mice rice

45

Page 46

Name _____   Skill: long i words -ive -ide

Write each word three times.

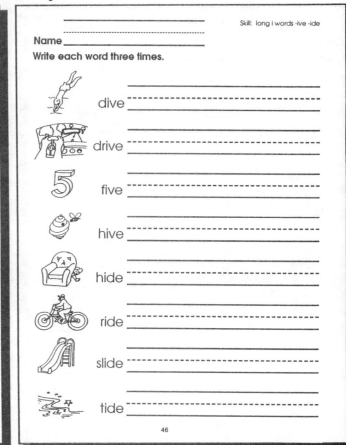

dive _____
drive _____
five _____
hive _____
hide _____
ride _____
slide _____
tide _____

46

Page 47

Name _____   Skill: long i words -ive -ide

Cut out the pictures. Match them to the words and paste.

tide   hive

drive   hide

ride   five

dive   slide

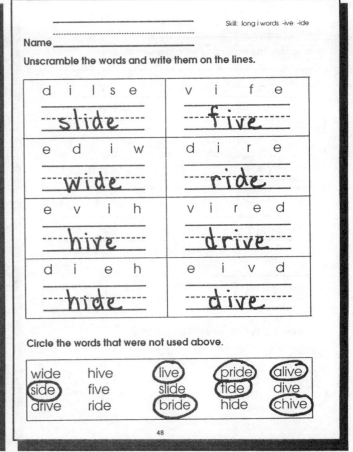

drive   hive   slide   ride

dive   five   tide   hide

47

Page 48

Name _____   Skill: long i words -ive -ide

Unscramble the words and write them on the lines.

d i l s e → **slide**	v i f e → **five**
e d i w → **wide**	d i r e → **ride**
e v i h → **hive**	v i r e d → **drive**
d i e h → **hide**	e i v d → **dive**

Circle the words that were not used above.

wide hive (live) (pride) (alive)
(side) five slide (tide) dive
drive ride (bride) hide (chive)

48

117   CD-3726

Answer Key

Name _____

Skill: long o words -oat -old

Write each word three times.

boat _____

coat _____

goat _____

moat _____

cold _____

fold _____

gold _____

hold _____

49

Name _____

Skill: long o words -o

Cut out the pictures. Match them to the words and paste.

gold   goat

boat   fold

hold   moat

coat   cold

coat	boat	goat	moat

hold   gold   cold   fold

50

Name _____

Skill: long o words -oat -old

Unscramble the words and write them on the lines.

t o c a	d o l f
coat	fold
a t o b	o a t m
boat	moat
o l d h	l o c d
hold	cold
t o a g	d o l g
goat	gold

Circle the words that were not used above.

(float)   gold   (oat)   moat   cold
boat   (told)   coat   hold   (bold)
(mold)   fold   goat   (sold) (old)

51

Name _____

Skill: long o words -one -ore

Write each word three times.

bone _____

cone _____

phone _____

stone _____

core _____

tore _____

shore _____

store _____

52

---

118   CD-3726

Answer Key

Name _____

Skill: long o words -one -ore

Cut out the pictures. Match them to the words and paste.

tore   phone

bone   store

core   stone

cone   shore

| tore | phone | store | cone |
| bone | stone 53 | shore | core |

Name _____

Skill: long o words -one -ore

Unscramble the words and write them on the lines.

n o p h e	r o c e
phone	core
o n c e	t r o e
cone	tore
s o h e r	o n s e t
shore	stone
o r t e s	n e o b
store	bone

Circle the words that were not used above.

bone	(more)	(pore)	(lore)	stone
core	cone	shore	(lone)	(tone)
phone	tore	(sore)	store	(bore)

54

Name _____

Skill: long u words u sound

Write each word three times.

cube _____

flute _____

fruit _____

fuel _____

huge _____

mule _____

music _____

ruler _____

55

Name _____

Skill: long u words u sound

Cut out the pictures. Match them to the words and paste.

fuel   flute

music   ruler

mule   cube

huge   fruit

| music | mule | fruit | flute |
| ruler | huge 56 | fuel | cube |

119
CD-3726

Name_____

Skill: long u words u sound

Unscramble the words and write them on the lines.

u h g e	l u e m
huge	mule
t i u f r	t u c e
fruit	cute
b c e u	s c u i m
cube	music
l e f u	l e r u r
fuel	ruler

Circle the words that were not used above.

fuel	cube	use	fruit	rule
fume	music	fuse	ruler	mule
future	cute	huge	fume	plume

57

Name_____

Skill: long u words oo sound

Write each word three times.

blue _____

cute _____

glue _____

prune _____

suit _____

super _____

tube _____

tune _____

58

Name_____

Skill: long u words oo sound

Cut out the pictures. Match them to the words and paste.

tune   glue

super   prune

blue   tube

cute   suit

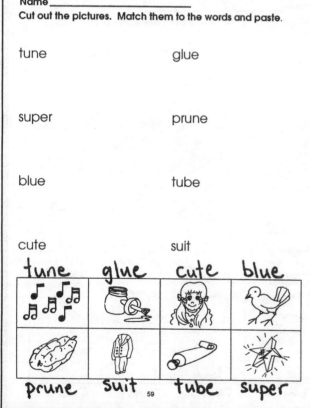

tune   glue   cute   blue

prune   suit   tube   super

59

Name_____

Skill: long u words oo sound

Unscramble the words and write them on the lines.

t n u e	u l g e
tune	gtue
p r u s e	n u p r e
super	prune
e u b l	u i t s
blue	suit
b u t e	t u f l e
tube	flute

Circle the words that were not used above.

flute	tung	ruin	glue	prune
dune	rude	tune	duty	future
suit	tube	blue	human	super

60

© 1996 Kelley Wingate Publications   120   CD-3726

Answer Key

_____
Skill: identify short vowel a e i o u

Name _____

Write the missing vowel for each picture.

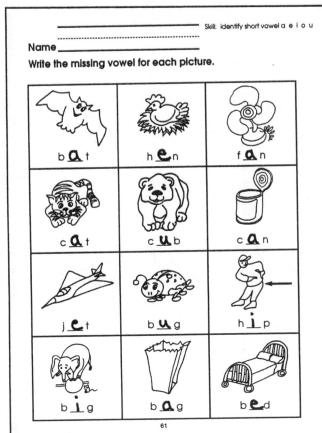

b **a** t	h **e** n	f **a** n
c **a** t	c **u** b	c **a** n
j **e** t	b **u** g	h **i** p
b **i** g	b **a** g	b **e** d

61

_____
Skill: identify short vowel a e i o u

Name _____

Write the missing vowel for each picture.

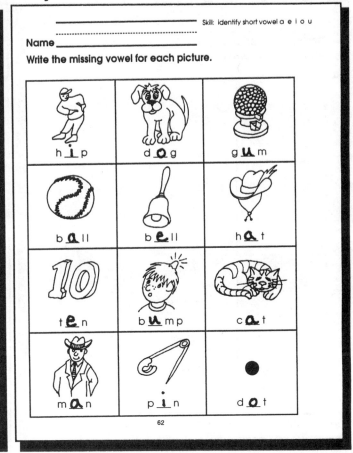

h **i** p	d **o** g	g **u** m
b **a** ll	b **e** ll	h **a** t
t **e** n	b **u** mp	c **a** t
m **a** n	p **i** n	d **o** t

62

_____
Skill: identify short vowel a e i o u

Name _____

Write the missing vowel for each picture.

r **u** b	f **a** n	n **e** t
d **o** g	m **o** p	j **u** g
r **a** g	f **e** d	l **i** p
h **o** g	dr **u** m	f **e** / **a** ll

63

_____
Skill: identify short vowel a e i o u

Name _____

Write the missing vowel for each picture.

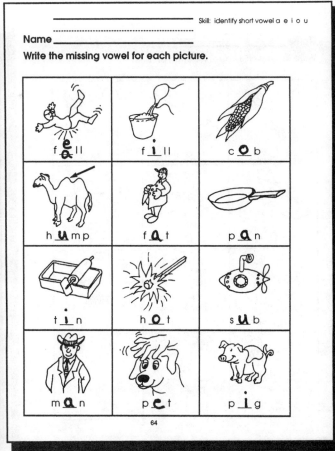

f **e** / **a** ll	f **i** ll	c **o** b
h **u** mp	f **a** t	p **a** n
t **i** n	h **o** t	s **u** b
m **a** n	p **e** t	p **i** g

64

121

CD-3726

Answer Key

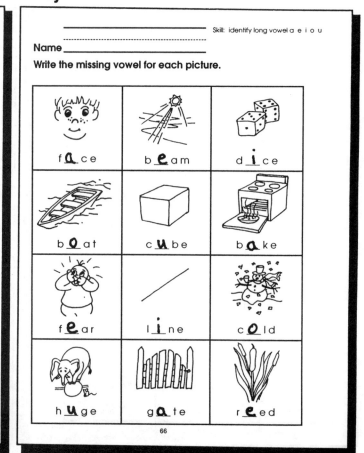

Skill: identify short vowel a e i o u

Name _____

Write the missing vowel for each picture.

p**o**p	r**u**g	t**a**g
r**e**d	r**i**p	j**u**g
m**u**m	t**a**ll	w**a**ll
h**i**ll	r**o**b	j**u**mp

65

Skill: identify long vowel a e i o u

Name _____

Write the missing vowel for each picture.

f**a**ce	b**e**am	d**i**ce
b**o**at	c**u**be	b**a**ke
f**e**ar	l**i**ne	c**o**ld
h**u**ge	g**a**te	r**e**ed

66

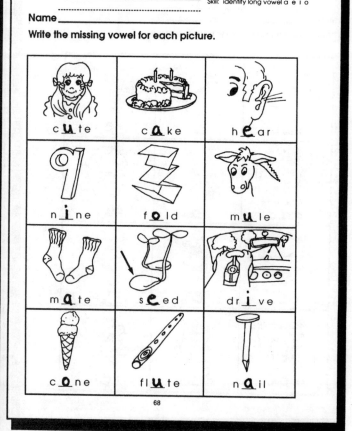

Skill: identify long vowel a e i o u

Name _____

Write the missing vowel for each picture.

d**i**ve	b**o**ne	bl**u**e
m**a**il	d**e**ep	h**i**de
c**o**re	s**u**it	l**a**ce
dr**e**am	m**i**ce	c**o**at

67

Skill: identify long vowel a e i o

Name _____

Write the missing vowel for each picture.

c**u**te	c**a**ke	h**e**ar
n**i**ne	f**o**ld	m**u**le
m**a**te	s**e**ed	dr**i**ve
c**o**ne	fl**u**te	n**a**il

68

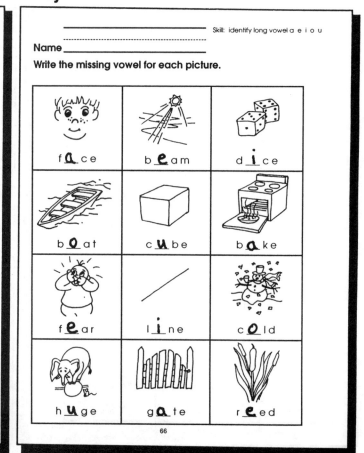

© 1996 Kelley Wingate Publications   122   CD-3726

Answer Key

Name _____

Write the missing vowel for each picture.

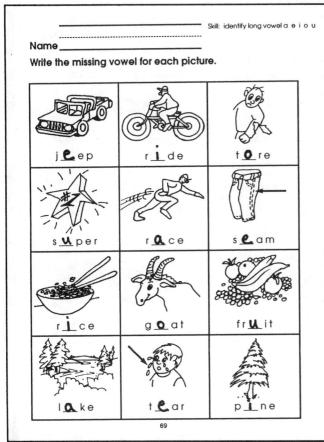

j**ee**p	r**i**de	t**o**re
s**u**per	r**a**ce	s**e**am
r**i**ce	g**o**at	fr**u**it
l**a**ke	t**e**ar	p**i**ne

69

Name _____

Write the missing vowel for each picture.

g**o**ld	m**u**sic	sp**ee**d
f**i**ve	ph**o**ne	gl**u**e
p**a**il	sh**ee**p	sl**i**de
c**o**re	t**u**be	pl**a**te

70

Name _____

Write the missing vowel for each picture.

w**i**n	sp**a**ce	p**o**t
t**e**am	t**u**b	pr**i**ce
p**a**n	m**o**at	w**e**t
f**ue**l	w**i**g	r**a**ke

71

Name _____

Write the missing vowel for each picture.

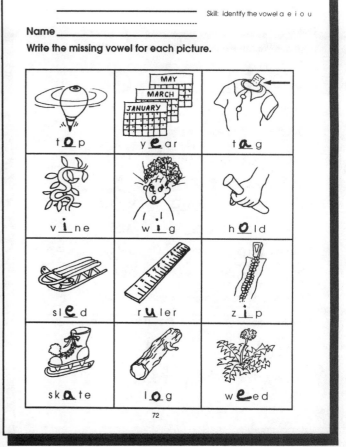

t**o**p	y**e**ar	t**a**g
v**i**ne	w**i**g	h**o**ld
sl**e**d	r**u**ler	z**i**p
sk**a**te	l**o**g	w**ee**d

72

---

123   CD-3726

Page 73

_____ Skill: identify the vowel a e i o u

Name _____

Write the missing vowel for each picture.

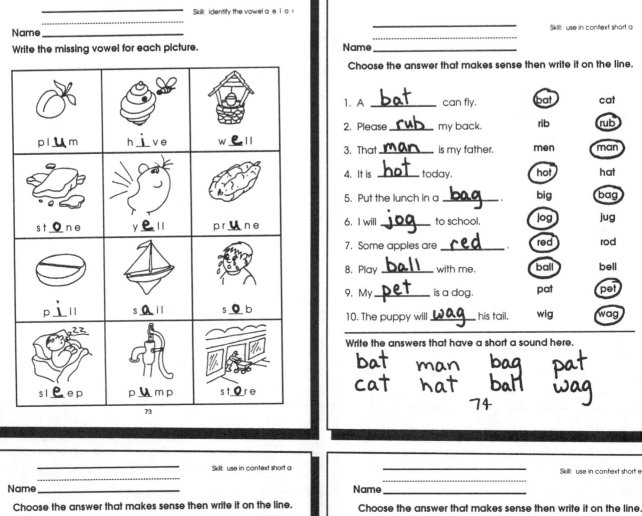

pl **u** m | h **i** v e | w **e** ll
st **o** ne | y **e** ll | pr **u** ne
p **i** ll | s **a** il | s **o** b
sl **e** ep | p **u** mp | st **o** re

73

Page 74

_____ Skill: use in context short a

Name _____

Choose the answer that makes sense then write it on the line.

1. A **bat** can fly. (bat) cat
2. Please **rub** my back. rib (rub)
3. That **man** is my father. men (man)
4. It is **hot** today. (hot) hat
5. Put the lunch in a **bag** . big (bag)
6. I will **jog** to school. (jog) jug
7. Some apples are **red** . (red) rod
8. Play **ball** with me. (ball) bell
9. My **pet** is a dog. pat (pet)
10. The puppy will **wag** his tail. wig (wag)

Write the answers that have a short a sound here.

bat   man   bag   pat
cat   hat   ball   wag
74

Page 75

_____ Skill: use in context short a

Name _____

Choose the answer that makes sense then write it on the line.

1. Do not **fall** down! (fall) fell
2. A fish has a **fin** . fun (fin)
3. A **rat** ate the cheese. sat (rat)
4. Do not **rip** my paper. (rip) lip
5. A **fan** makes wind. fin (fan)
6. A camel has one **hump** . (hump) jump
7. A rabbit can **hop** . (hop) hip
8. I can **dig** a big hole. (dig) dug
9. I play a **drum** in the band. gum (drum)
10. I will **win** the race. won (win)

Write the answers that have a short a sound here.

fall   rat
sat   fan
75

Page 76

_____ Skill: use in context short e

Name _____

Choose the answer that makes sense then write it on the line.

1. The **rug** is on the floor. (rug) rag
2. Are you feeling **well** ? (well) will
3. That is a **tall** tree. tell (tall)
4. A **jet** flys over clouds. jot (jet)
5. The **hen** has two chicks. (hen) men
6. Spot is the name of my **dog** . dig (dog)
7. I got **wet** in the rain. (wet) met
8. **Fill** my cup to the top. (Fill) Fall
9. I will go to **bed** now. (bed) bad
10. Fry the eggs in that **pan** . pin (pan)

Write the answers that have a short e sound here.

well   jet   men   met
tell   hen   wet   bed
76

Answer Key

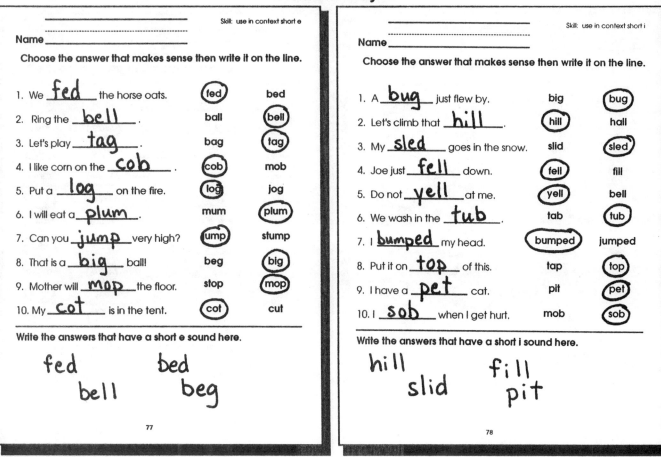

Name _____
Skill: use in context short e

Choose the answer that makes sense then write it on the line.

1. We **fed** the horse oats. — (fed)   bed
2. Ring the **bell** . — ball   (bell)
3. Let's play **tag** . — bag   (tag)
4. I like corn on the **cob** . — (cob)   mob
5. Put a **log** on the fire. — (log)   jog
6. I will eat a **plum** . — mum   (plum)
7. Can you **jump** very high? — (jump)   stump
8. That is a **big** ball! — beg   (big)
9. Mother will **mop** the floor. — stop   (mop)
10. My **cot** is in the tent. — (cot)   cut

Write the answers that have a short e sound here.

fed   bed
   bell   beg

77

Name _____
Skill: use in context short i

Choose the answer that makes sense then write it on the line.

1. A **bug** just flew by. — big   (bug)
2. Let's climb that **hill** . — (hill)   hall
3. My **sled** goes in the snow. — slid   (sled)
4. Joe just **fell** down. — (fell)   fill
5. Do not **yell** at me. — (yell)   bell
6. We wash in the **tub** . — tab   (tub)
7. I **bumped** my head. — (bumped)   jumped
8. Put it on **top** of this. — tap   (top)
9. I have a **pet** cat. — pit   (pet)
10. I **sob** when I get hurt. — mob   (sob)

Write the answers that have a short i sound here.

hill   fill
   slid   pit

78

Name _____
Skill: use in context short o

Choose the answer that makes sense then write it on the line.

1. A **pill** can make you well. — hill   (pill)
2. Put a **dot** over the letter i. — pot   (dot)
3. The dog **tugs** on a rope. — bugs   (tugs)
4. **Zip** the zipper. — (Zip)   Sip
5. A **hip** is part of a leg. — (hip)   hop
6. This old shirt is a **rag** . — (rag)   rig
7. I have **ten** toes. — tin   (ten)
8. I like to drink **pop** . — pup   (pop)
9. Cook soup in a big **pot** . — pet   (pot)
10. That lady wears a **wig** . — wag   (wig)

Write the answers that have a short o sound here.

pot   hop
dot   pop   pot

79

Name _____
Skill: use in context short u

Choose the answer that makes sense then write it on the line.

1. A **pig** is an animal. — (pig)   peg
2. I bit my **lip** ! — lap   (lip)
3. A **mum** is a flower. — (mum)   gum
4. A **cub** is a baby bear. — (cub)   cab
5. Boys grow up to be **men** . — (men)   hen
6. I blow bubbles with **gum** . — (gum)   hum
7. I have a butterfly **net** . — (net)   nut
8. Use a **pen** , not a pencil. — ten   (pen)
9. A **sub** goes under water. — sob   (sub)
10. **Pump** air into my bike tires. — (Pump)   Lump

Write the answers that have a short u sound here.

mum   cub   hum   sub   Lump
gum   gum   nut   Pump

80

Answer Key

Name _____

Skill: use in context long a

Choose the answer that makes sense then write it on the line.

1. __Nail__ the wood together. Sail (Nail)
2. Leaves grow on a __vine__. mine (vine)
3. __Seeds__ grow into plants. Needs (Seeds)
4. __Bake__ the cake in the oven. (Bake) Bike
5. The ice cream is __cold__. (cold) fold
6. The __phone__ is ringing. cone (phone)
7. I like __rice__ with my dinner. race (rice)
8. You did a __super__ job! (super) fruit
9. Put your food on a __plate__. gate (plate)
10. Let's have a __race__. face (race)

Write the answers that have a long a sound here.

Sail Bake gate face
Nail race plate race

81

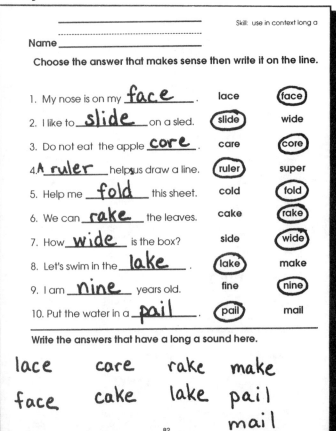

Name _____

Skill: use in context long a

Choose the answer that makes sense then write it on the line.

1. My nose is on my __face__. lace (face)
2. I like to __slide__ on a sled. (slide) wide
3. Do not eat the apple __core__. care (core)
4. A __ruler__ helps us draw a line. (ruler) super
5. Help me __fold__ this sheet. cold (fold)
6. We can __rake__ the leaves. cake (rake)
7. How __wide__ is the box? side (wide)
8. Let's swim in the __lake__. (lake) make
9. I am __nine__ years old. fine (nine)
10. Put the water in a __pail__. (pail) mail

Write the answers that have a long a sound here.

lace care rake make
face cake lake pail
                      mail

82

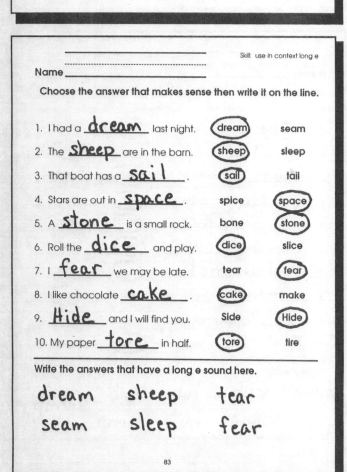

Name _____

Skill: use in context long e

Choose the answer that makes sense then write it on the line.

1. I had a __dream__ last night. (dream) seam
2. The __sheep__ are in the barn. (sheep) sleep
3. That boat has a __sail__. (sail) tail
4. Stars are out in __space__. spice (space)
5. A __stone__ is a small rock. bone (stone)
6. Roll the __dice__ and play. (dice) slice
7. I __fear__ we may be late. tear (fear)
8. I like chocolate __cake__. (cake) make
9. __Hide__ and I will find you. Side (Hide)
10. My paper __tore__ in half. (tore) tire

Write the answers that have a long e sound here.

dream sheep tear
seam sleep fear

83

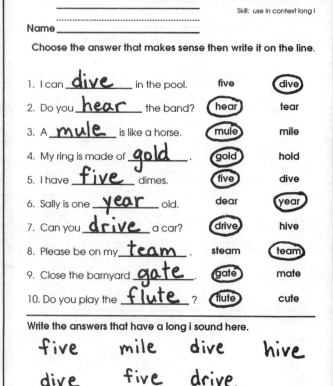

Name _____

Skill: use in context long i

Choose the answer that makes sense then write it on the line.

1. I can __dive__ in the pool. five (dive)
2. Do you __hear__ the band? (hear) tear
3. A __mule__ is like a horse. (mule) mile
4. My ring is made of __gold__. (gold) hold
5. I have __five__ dimes. (five) dive
6. Sally is one __year__ old. dear (year)
7. Can you __drive__ a car? (drive) hive
8. Please be on my __team__. steam (team)
9. Close the barnyard __gate__. (gate) mate
10. Do you play the __flute__? (flute) cute

Write the answers that have a long i sound here.

five mile dive hive
dive five drive

84

126 CD-3726

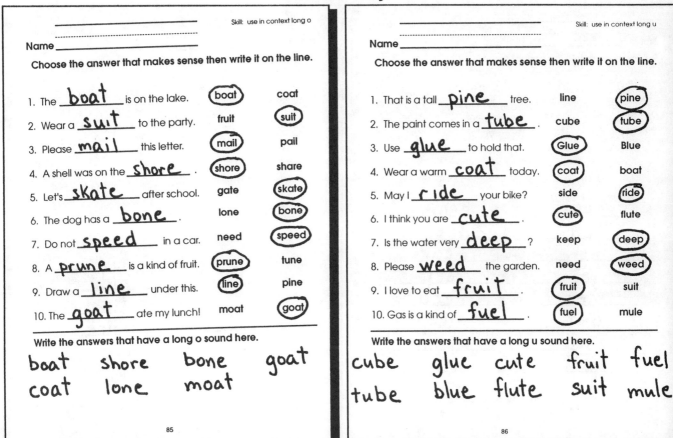

Page 85

Skill: use in context long o

Name _____

Choose the answer that makes sense then write it on the line.

1. The **boat** is on the lake. (boat) coat
2. Wear a **suit** to the party. fruit (suit)
3. Please **mail** this letter. (mail) pail
4. A shell was on the **shore**. (shore) share
5. Let's **skate** after school. gate (skate)
6. The dog has a **bone**. lone (bone)
7. Do not **speed** in a car. need (speed)
8. A **prune** is a kind of fruit. (prune) tune
9. Draw a **line** under this. (line) pine
10. The **goat** ate my lunch! moat (goat)

Write the answers that have a long o sound here.

boat   shore   bone   goat
coat   lone   moat

85

Page 86

Skill: use in context long u

Name _____

Choose the answer that makes sense then write it on the line.

1. That is a tall **pine** tree. line (pine)
2. The paint comes in a **tube**. cube (tube)
3. Use **glue** to hold that. (Glue) Blue
4. Wear a warm **coat** today. (coat) boat
5. May I **ride** your bike? side (ride)
6. I think you are **cute**. (cute) flute
7. Is the water very **deep**? keep (deep)
8. Please **weed** the garden. need (weed)
9. I love to eat **fruit**. (fruit) suit
10. Gas is a kind of **fuel**. (fuel) mule

Write the answers that have a long u sound here.

cube   glue   cute   fruit   fuel
tube   blue   flute   suit   mule

86

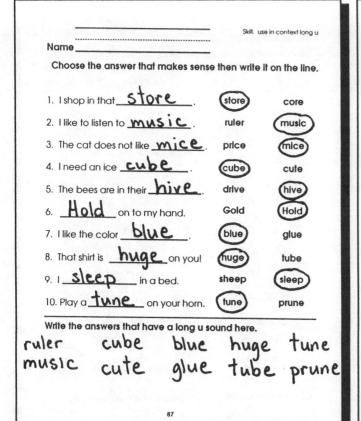

Page 87

Skill: use in context long u

Name _____

Choose the answer that makes sense then write it on the line.

1. I shop in that **store**. (store) core
2. I like to listen to **music**. ruler (music)
3. The cat does not like **mice**. price (mice)
4. I need an ice **cube**. (cube) cute
5. The bees are in their **hive**. drive (hive)
6. **Hold** on to my hand. Gold (Hold)
7. I like the color **blue**. (blue) glue
8. That shirt is **huge** on you! (huge) tube
9. I **sleep** in a bed. sheep (sleep)
10. Play a **tune** on your horn. (tune) prune

Write the answers that have a long u sound here.

ruler   cube   blue   huge   tune
music   cute   glue   tube   prune

87

Page 88

Skill: categorize long and short a

Name _____

Put these words into the correct group.

bag   bat   bake   cake
can   fan   face   gate
mate   nail   pan   rag
rake   space   tall   wall

Short a	Long a
bag	bake
bat	cake
can	face
fan	gate
pan	mate
rag	nail
tall	rake
wall	space

Choose five words and draw a picture next to each.

88

Answer Key

Skill: categorize long and short e

Name _____

Put these words into the correct group.

beam	bed	deep	fear
fell	hen	jeep	jet
men	pet	reed	sled
sleep	team	year	yell

Short e	Long e
bed	beam
fell	deep
hen	fear
jet	jeep
men	reed
pet	sleep
sled	team
yell	year

Choose five words and draw a picture next to each.

89

Skill: categorize long and short i

Name _____

Put these words into the correct group.

bill	dice	dig	dive
fin	five	hide	hill
line	lip	pin	price
vine	wide	wig	zip

Short i	Long i
bill	dice
dig	dive
fin	five
hill	hide
lip	line
pin	price
wig	vine
zip	wide

Choose five words and draw a picture next to each.

90

Skill: categorize long and short o

Name _____

Put these words into the correct group.

boat	cob	cone	dot
fold	goat	hold	hop
jog	log	moat	mop
phone	pot	rob	store

Short o	Long o
cob	boat
dot	cone
hop	fold
jog	goat
log	hold
mop	moat
pot	phone
rob	store

Choose five words and draw a picture next to each.

91

Skill: categorize long and short u

Name _____

Put these words into the correct group.

blue	bug	cub	cute
drum	flute	fruit	glue
gum	hump	jug	mule
rub	ruler	tug	tune

Short u	Long u
bug	blue
cub	cute
drum	flute
gum	fruit
hump	glue
jug	mule
rub	ruler
tug	tune

Choose five words and draw a picture next to each.

92

Answer Key

Page 93

Name _____
Skill: categorize long/short a/e

Put these words into the correct group.

ball	bell	cat	dream
fed	hear	lake	man
net	pail	race	sheep
skate	ten	wag	weed

Short a
ball
cat
man
wag

Long a
lake
pail
race
skate

Short e
bell
fed
net
ten

Long e
dream
hear
sheep
weed

93

Page 94

Name _____
Skill: categorize long/short o/u

Put these words into the correct group.

bone	bump	coat	core
cot	cube	dog	huge
mule	plum	rug	sob
stone	suit	top	tub

Short o
cot
dog
sob
top

Long o
bone
coat
core
stone

Short u
bump
plum
rug
tub

Long u
cube
huge
mule
suit

94

Page 95

Name _____
Skill: context short a

Fill in the blanks with the short a words in the box.

Sally's Walk

Sally went for a walk down her street. She stopped in front of the house next to hers. A **man** was in the yard. He was feeding his **cat**. The man went into his house. The cat jumped to the top of a brick **wall** that went around the yard. Sally walked on to the next yard. A dog was barking at the cat. He began to **wag** his tail when he saw Sally. He got his **ball** and tossed it in the air. The dog put the ball at Sally's feet and **sat** down. She threw the ball and the dog went after it. He came back with a paper **bag** in his mouth. A **tag** on the bag said "Open Me". He gave the bag to **Sally** and she opened it. **Can** you guess what was inside?

bag	ball	Can	cat	man
Sally	sat	tag	wag	wall

95

Page 96

Name _____
Skill: context short e

Fill in the blanks with the short e words at the bottom of the page.

Ned

One summer day Ned went to his uncle's farm. He went to the barnyard to look around. Ned saw a fat **hen** and her five babies. He **fed** corn to the hen. There were some sheep in a **pen** near the barn. A horse and her colt were in the barn. Ned stopped to **pet** the soft nose of the colt. Ned walked out of the barn and saw a round stone wall. He looked over the wall and saw that it was a wishing **well**. Ned bent over to see further into the well and **fell** in! The water was not very deep, but Ned was all **wet**. He began to **yell** for help. Two **men** came running. They used a big **net** to pull him out. Ned laughed and said "I am all right now"!

fed	fell	hen	men	net
pen	pet	well	wet	yell

96

Answer Key

Name

Skill: context short i

Name

Fill in the blanks with the short i words **at the bottom of the page.**

Bill's Pond

Bill was playing in his back yard. He saw a **big** pile of dirt under a bush. It was an ant **hill**. He had an idea. He would make a pond for the ants to **swim** in. The ants could race and see who would **win**. Bill began to **dig** a small hole next to the ant hill. He worked on that hole for a long time. When it was ready he **filled** the hole with water. The ants came to the pond but they did not go **in**. Bill laughed at his **silly** idea. Ants cannot swim. They do not have **fins** like fish. But now they have a nice pond to look at!

big	dig	filled	fins	hill
in	silly	swim	will	win

97

Skill: context short o

Name

Fill in the blanks with the short o words **at the bottom of the page.**

Friends

Bob and Rob are friends. They are alike in many ways. Both boys like to climb to the **top** of the fence. Then they **hop** down. They both have a **dog** for a pet. They even like the same foods. Their favorite food is corn on the **cob**. Bob and Rob like to drink **hot** chocolate in the winter and cold **pop** in the summer. Both boys like to make things. Once they made a big **pot** out of clay. Another time they made a **log** cabin out of sticks. Bob and **Rob** have known each other since they were two years old. They have been friends for a **long** time!

cob	dog	hop	hot	log
long	pop	pot	Rob	top

98

Skill: context short u

Name

Fill in the blanks with the short u words **at the bottom of the page.**

My Toy Box

I have a big box to keep my toys in. It is painted yellow and green. My box is **full** of toys. At the bottom I keep an old red **drum** for banging. Next I have three boats and one **sub** to play with in the **tub**. On top of them I keep two stuffed animals. One is a camel with a big **hump**. The other is a small bear **cub**. On the top I keep a real animal! It is a **bug** with wings and six legs. My toy box is so full I have to **tug** on the top to open it. Sometimes I pull the top so hard it flies open and **bumps** my head. Then I have to **rub** my head to make it feel better.

bug	bumps	cub	drum	full
hump	rub	sub	tub	tug

99

Skill: context long a

Name

Fill in the blanks with the long a words **at the bottom of the page.**

Amy's Party

Amy is having a party today. She **mailed** letters to all her friends last week to tell them about it. Amy has put on her best dress. It has **lace** all over it. Her mother has **baked** a **cake** for the children to eat. They will put the cake on party **plates**. Amy has **made** many plans for her party. The children will play **games**. They will have a running **race**. They may even **sail** boats on the nearby pond! The doorbell rings. It is the first guest. Amy has a big smile on her **face**.

baked	cake	face	games	lace
made	mailed	plates	race	sail

100

CD-3726

Answer Key

Name_____

Skill: context long e

Fill in the blanks with the long e words at the bottom of the page.

A Dream by the Sea

Last week Lee went camping with her family. They went to a camp by the sea. They knew it was a nice place because they went there last **year**. The camp has a nice beach for swimming. **Lee** likes to swim in water that is not too **deep**. She is not a good swimmer. The family likes to camp by the **sea**. They have a **jeep** to drive over the sand dunes. They **sleep** in a tent. Lee likes to **hear** the waves at night. One night she had a **dream**. She found a large **seed** and planted it. A giant **weed** grew from the seed. It became a sea weed. What a strange dream!

dream	deep	hear	jeep	Lee
sea	seed	sleep	weed	year

101

Name_____

Skill: context long i

Fill in the blanks with the long i words at the bottom of the page.

The Woods

Mike and Ivan like to picnic in the woods. It takes them only **five** minutes to get there. They like to **ride** their **bikes** down the trails. There are many **pine** trees in the woods. Some of them are covered with **vines** that are just right for swinging from. One tree is so **wide** the boys cannot put their arms around it! Mike and Ivan like to **hide** in the bushes and watch for animals. They often see little **mice** gathering seeds. Once they saw some bees going into a large **hive**. The woods are **alive** with small animals that are fun to watch.

alive	bikes	five	hide	hive
pine	mice	ride	vines	wide

102

Name_____

Skill: context long o

Fill in the blanks with the long o words at the bottom of the page.

Gold Fish

Once a boy named Joe lived near a castle. There was a **moat** around the castle and Joe liked to fish there. He had a small **boat** to fish from. The boat **floated** on the water as Joe fished. **Joe** caught one fish each day for his dinner. One winter morning it was very **cold** out. Joe put on his **coat** and went to the moat. His fingers were so cold he could barely **hold** the oars. He pushed away from the **shore** and began to fish. He looked down and saw a shiny **stone** in the water. Joe picked it up and saw that it was a big piece of **gold**. He had found gold instead of a fish. What a lucky day!

boat	coat	cold	floated	gold
hold	Joe	moat	shore	stone

103

Name_____

Skill: context long u

Fill in the blanks with the long u words at the bottom of the page.

Ruth's Flute

Ruth likes school. She loves **music** class better than anything. She plays a **flute** in the band. Her teacher says she is a **super** student. She can play a **tune** without looking at the music! **Ruth** is learning to write her own songs. She uses a **ruler** to make the lines then draws in the notes. Ruth will play at a school program tonight. She puts on her best **suit** so she will look nice. It is the color of a **blue** sky. Her father says she looks **cute**. There is a **huge** crowd at the school. Ruth plays well and everyone claps.

blue	cute	flute	huge	music
ruler	Ruth	suit	super	tune

104

131

CD-3726

Certificate of Completion

This certificate certifies that

Has completed

Signed

Date

Keep up the Great Work!

earns this award for

You are TERRIFIC!

Signed

Date

Great Success!

_____

earns this award for

_____

I am Proud of You!

Signed _____

Date _____

You Did It!

earns this award for

_____

Keep Up The The Great Work!

_____   _____
Signed   Date

Congratulations!

Receives this award for

_____

Keep up the great work!

_____

Signed

Date

Great Job!

Receives this award for

_____

Keep up the great work!

_____
Signed

_____
Date

Keep up the Great Work!

_____ earns this award for _____

You are TERRIFIC!

Signed _____

Date _____